Working with Groups of Friends

Working with GROUPS of FRIENDS

Teresa Whitfield

United States Institute of Peace
Washington, D.C.

The Peacemaker's Toolkit Series Editors: A. Heather Coyne and Nigel Quinney

The views expressed in this guide are those of the author alone. They do not necessarily reflect views of the United States Institute of Peace.

United States Institute of Peace
1200 17th Street NW, Suite 200
Washington, DC 20036-3011

Phone: 202-457-1700
Fax: 202-429-6063
E-mail: usip_requests@usip.org
Web: www.usip.org

© 2010 by the Endowment of the United States Institute of Peace and Mediation Support Project. All rights reserved.

First published 2010.

To request permission to photocopy or reprint materials for course use, contact Copyright Clearance Center at www.copyright.com.

Printed in the United States of America

The paper used in this publication meets the minimum requirements of American National Standards for Information Science Permanence of Paper for Printed Library Materials, ANSI Z39.48-1984.

Library of Congress Cataloging-in-Publication Data

Whitfield, Teresa.
  Working with groups of friends / Teresa Whitfield.
    p. cm. — (The peacemaker's toolkit series)
  Includes bibliographical references.
  ISBN 978-1-60127-059-7 (pbk. : alk. paper)
  1. Peace-building—International cooperation. 2. Conflict management--International cooperation. 3. Mediation, International. I. United States Institute of Peace. II. Title.
    JZ5538.W48 2010
    327.1'72--dc22

Contents

Introduction 5

Step 1: Assess the Environment for Friends 13

Step 2: Develop a Strategy 23

Step 3: Engage with Friends and Conflict Parties 41

Step 4: Sustain Coordinated Support 51

Step 5: Prepare for Implementation 63

Conclusion 71

Notes 73

Acknowledgments 75

About the Author 76

About the United States Institute of Peace 77

Introduction

How to work with the many external actors involved in any peace process is a critical issue for peacemakers. As conflict resolution activity has surged in the years since the end of the Cold War, mediators and others have developed a wide array of new arrangements to address this challenge. Most notable among them are informal mini-coalitions of states or intergovernmental organizations that provide support for resolving conflicts and implementing peace agreements—an innovation often referred to as groups of "Friends." [1]

Between 1990 and 2009, "Friends," "contact groups," "core groups," and other such mechanisms—many of them established to support or work alongside UN peacemaking and peace operations—mushroomed from four to more than thirty, a larger than sevenfold increase. Although some groups were formed on the initiative of mediators, others were self-selecting, or even assembled by the conflict parties themselves. They all understood that a peace process would benefit from a unified effort on its behalf. Peacemakers' experiences of these groups illustrated the elusiveness of such unity among the various external actors—neighbors, regional and more distant powers, donors, and other interested states—but also how important unity is.

With an emphasis on the small groups of states or intergovernmental organizations that are gathered as "Friends" of a mediator or a particular process (but that are not themselves leading the mediation or negotiation), this volume seeks to explore how peacemakers may most productively work with groups of Friends. It takes as a starting point that a group of Friends is an auxiliary mechanism, engaged in the service of a wider strategy for peace—not a substitute for one. As an auxiliary device, a group of Friends cannot create the conditions for peace, but it can contribute to their emergence in a variety of ways.

This handbook draws on the mixed experiences of peacemakers with groups of Friends. It cautions that Friends will not be desirable in every peace process or, necessary, in a similar form at every stage of a peace process. Friends can help marshal leverage, resources, coordination, and expertise in a mediator's support. But there are also circumstances—usually related to a lack of compatibility between the interests of the states concerned and the overall demands of the process—in which Friends may prove a complicating factor. A mediator may, after careful analysis, decide that he or she is better off without them.

Where Friends Are Found

Friends have most frequently been involved in efforts to resolve internal armed conflicts waged between a state and one or more nonstate parties. Beyond this general observation, it is difficult to draw conclusions about their occurrence on the basis either of geography or of the type of conflict with which they have been engaged.

Whether initially convened by a lead mediator or not, Friends are essentially self-selecting: their sustained involvement is the result of their significant interest in a peace process. Perhaps paradoxically, it is also an indication of the absence of an overriding interest in a conflict's outcome on the part of the major powers. These powers are not likely to relinquish a driving role in conflicts at the top of the international agenda to an informal group of states working in support of a third-party peacemaker. Policy toward the Balkans, the Middle East, Iraq, and Afghanistan, for example, has been driven by direct diplomacy by the powers most immediately involved, acting bilaterally, if at times through structures such as the Contact Group on the former Yugoslavia (France, Germany, Italy, Russia, the United Kingdom, and the United States) and the Quartet on the Middle East (the European Union, Russia, the United States, and the United Nations).

Geography is not the only determining factor in the formation of groups of Friends. Yet certain geographic tendencies can be identified as favoring their formation. The perceived success of the early use of Friends in Central America has made such mechanisms popular in Latin America as a whole. By contrast, a relatively low incidence of UN peace operations in Asia, Europe, and the Middle East made those regions less likely to turn to Friends groups. In Africa, meanwhile, the concerted effort toward a more collaborative approach to peace and security adopted by the African Union has boosted the popularity of groups of all kinds, not just groups of Friends.

Friends have been present in conflicts recognizably "easier" than others to settle, such as those in Central America. They have also been present in some of the most intractable (Georgia-Abkhazia, Colombia, and Cyprus, for example), involving issues of territory as well as government and sustained by both ideology and illicit resources. Like other peacemaking initiatives they have struggled to exert an impact in circumstances—such as a secessionist conflict—in which the parties pursue a zero-sum option. They have rarely been engaged in the most violent phases of a conflict, nor have they played a prominent role in resolving many of the most deadly conflicts of the post–Cold War period (such as Rwanda, the Democratic Republic of Congo [DRC], or the Balkans).

A number of the conflicts that have not seen a Friends group form have involved complex regional dynamics or considerable differences among the outside powers that have discouraged the formation of groups. This underlines the fact that whether a group of Friends will be present in a conflict relates less to the internal characteristics of the conflict and more to external actors' interests and the agency of a few key individuals.

The Challenges of Conceptual Clarity

An attempt to distinguish among the many Friends, Core, Contact, and other groups that have proliferated in the post–Cold War period is complicated by the differences among them that their titles do little to explain. The various groups have differed in the circumstances of their creation, in the mix of their members, and in their functions. Different relationships have formed between the lead mediator and involved states. And different groups have had widely different impacts on the broad range of conflicts with which they have been engaged. In several cases, groups have varied considerably during the period of their engagement as a consequence of changes in their composition and functions or have been complemented by supplementary mechanisms.

This handbook introduces a rough typology (elaborated in Step Two) that distinguishes among Friends of the mediator or process, ad hoc arrangements, contact groups, implementation and monitoring groups, and assistance coordination groups. The first two of these are those of most immediate concern to a peacemaker involved in the early stages of a peace process. They represent structures or arrangements that will be directly affected by the quality of a mediator's engagement. Clearly, what each group or arrangement may be able to offer will depend on both the specific requirements of the conflict at hand, and the characteristics, capacities, and resources of its membership.

A range of variables may either help or impede the peacemaker's efforts to develop an effective strategy for the involvement of external actors. Whatever structure is deemed appropriate, it will likely involve attention to how to make best use of external partners' leverage, knowledge, and resources; how to block or neutralize unhelpful external involvement; and how to build and sustain broad-based support for an eventual settlement.

Friends and Outcomes

The variety of elements necessary for groups of Friends to form and perform works against assumptions regarding their causal relationship to the outcome of a process. However, a comparative analysis of groups of Friends and other informal structures points to several factors that contribute to the likelihood of their success: the *regional environment* in which the conflict takes place; the *conflict parties'* demands, practices, and interactions with the various third parties mediating or in a group structure; a group's *composition* and the resources that this may bring with it; questions of *leadership* encompassing a group's relationship with the lead peacemaker or mediator, be it a representative of the UN secretary-general, individual state, or nongovernmental peacemaker; and *timing* or the *phase of the process* with which the group is involved.

► The importance of the *regional environment* to the success of a peace process is widely acknowledged.[2] Indeed, it is difficult to cite examples of the sustainable resolution of a conflict in situations in which regional actors have not lent their support. Unsurprisingly, conflicts at the heart of complex regional conflicts, such as those that take place in the shadow of the pronounced interests of a larger and more powerful neighbor, have generally been without Friends. But where the regional environment is more conducive to the settlement of a conflict, Friends or other groups have been highly effective in engaging regional actors, some of which may also assume responsibilities for mediation.

➤ In considering the conditions needed for the successful involvement of group structures, the nature of the *conflict parties* emerges as more significant than the type of conflict. Individual members of Friends and other groups are generally representatives of governments with bilateral relations with the governments involved, often with clearly held positions on the issues at stake. As such, they may encounter problems in engaging directly with nonstate armed actors.[3] In countering this bias, critical factors for constructive engagement include the nonstate actors' demands (ideological, decolonialist, or secessionist), practices (more or less abusive of human rights, profiting from illicit resources, or identified as "terrorist"), and the degree of international engagement they have pursued in the conflict and efforts to end it (bringing with it the potential for leverage by third parties).

➤ The *composition* of any group is all-important. As with its formation, a group's composition is directly related to the strategic purposes pursued by its architects, and the distinct contributions made within each process by different Friends and kinds of Friends. In most cases, a small size is seen as key to a group's efficacy. Groups formed at the United Nations have generally been a mix of permanent members of the Security Council, interested regional actors, and midsize donor states or "helpful fixers" with experience of the conflict. Such a mix brings the promise of various resources to the table, which may include diplomatic leverage with one or more of the conflict parties, financial assistance for relief and reconstruction, and the commitment of troops in a UN peace operation or alongside it. In all cases, the essential prerequisite is that group members hold the settlement of the conflict as their highest goal.

➤ Issues of *leadership* go to the heart of what or whom Friends or other group structures are created for. In cases in which the United Nations has the lead in the peacemaking effort, groups have engaged with differing levels of collaboration with the secretary-general or the senior official representing him in a peace process. In some circumstances, a group has helped to bridge the gap between the fragile independence of the secretary-general and the power politics of the Security Council. In other processes, however, this has not proved possible, and states' conflicting interests have complicated the relationship between the secretary-general or his representative and groups of Friends. Peacemaking conducted outside the United Nations or with the United Nations in a supporting role—which has become increasingly common in recent years—underlines the importance of having coherent leadership. Indeed, who or what organization exercises leadership is less important than the degree of coherence with which that leadership is exercised.

► The *timing* of a group's formation and/or the *phase of the process* with which it is involved have had a central bearing on both a group's functions and impact in a given process, as distinct operational needs have led to varied relationships among the actors involved. Most obviously, the relationship between the mediator and a group of Friends that has been involved in peacemaking will change with the signing of an agreement and the establishment of a peace operation to monitor or assist in its implementation. Whether the Security Council mandates such an operation or not, peacebuilding will require the allocation, commitment, and coordination of resources that are likely to benefit from structures established in its support.

The Structure of This Handbook

This volume, like other handbooks in the *Peacemaker's Toolkit* series, draws on the lessons to be learned from both more and less successful examples of peacemaking. It introduces five specific steps for mediators considering working with groups of Friends: (1) assess the environment for Friends, (2) develop a strategy, (3) engage with Friends and conflict parties, (4) sustain coordinated support, and (5) prepare for implementation. Although these steps are presented sequentially, once begun, some steps will be ongoing and necessarily overlap with others.

This handbook—which is about working with groups of Friends—may appear to assume the presence or formation of such a group, but it does not advocate for their creation. Rather, this handbook seeks to help mediators both weigh the pros and cons of Friends, as one among the options that may be before them, and work more productively with them, whether they have a hand in selecting Friends themselves, or find Friends wished upon them.

Introduction

The Peacemaker's Toolkit

This handbook is part of the series *The Peacemaker's Toolkit,* which is being published by the United States Institute of Peace.

For twenty-five years, the United States Institute of Peace has supported the work of mediators through research, training programs, workshops, and publications designed to discover and disseminate the keys to effective mediation. The Institute—mandated by the U.S. Congress to help prevent, manage, and resolve international conflict through nonviolent means—has conceived of *The Peacemaker's Toolkit* as a way of combining its own accumulated expertise with that of other organizations active in the field of mediation. Most publications in the series are produced jointly by the Institute and a partner organization. All publications are carefully reviewed before publication by highly experienced mediators to ensure that the final product will be a useful and reliable resource for practitioners.

The Online Version

There is an online version of *The Peacemaker's Toolkit* that presents not only the text of this handbook but also connects readers to a vast web of information. Links in the online version give readers immediate access to a considerable variety of publications, news reports, directories, and other sources of data regarding ongoing mediation initiatives, case studies, theoretical frameworks, and education and training. These links enable the online *Toolkit* to serve as a "you are here" map to the larger literature on mediation.

STEP ONE

Assess the Environment for Friends

Just as the first step in any mediation effort is to assess the conflict, so, in thinking about groups of Friends, the first step must be to assess the environment for Friends within the broader exercise of conflict analysis. This will involve critical reflection upon a mediator's own strengths and weaknesses as well as considered attention to the potential Friends, external actors from which the mediator may seek support in his or her interactions with the conflict parties.

Consider the Mediation's Strengths and Weaknesses

Track-I mediators become involved with a conflict on the basis of different levels of visibility, legitimacy, and authority. They bring with them varying capacities for engaging with conflict parties, as well as quite distinct relations with other external actors with an interest in, or influence over, a given conflict. The nature and provenance of the mediator will therefore have a direct effect on whether a group of Friends is desirable and, if so, how it should be formed.

Different Mediators

Recent years have seen both a dramatic growth in mediation and an unprecedented diversity of mediators. This reflects two distinct shifts. One is a move away from mediations that are led exclusively by the United Nations and great powers and a move toward an increase in responsibility on the part of regional organizations and states. The other shift is a growth in the involvement of independent international mediators (such as the Centre for Humanitarian Dialogue and the Community of Sant'Egidio) and prestigious individuals. These individuals sometimes run their own organizations (former president of Finland Martti Ahtisaari heads the Conflict Management Initiative; former U.S. president Jimmy Carter, the Carter Center; and former UN secretary-general Kofi Annan, his own foundation).

Different mediators—the United Nations, regional and subregional organizations, individual states, private peacemakers, and prestigious individuals—will engage with external actors, and can contemplate working with groups of Friends. Each of these mediators will have a distinct perspective.

- A UN mediator works with the advantages of the organization's legitimacy and operational breadth. The support of UN member states is a critical element of the organization's efficacy as a mediator. Without it, the leverage and resources of the secretary-general would be limited. However, a UN mediator is also subject to pressures from individual states, both when they are parties to a conflict and when they are external actors with strong views about how a given conflict should be approached.

- Regional and subregional organizations mediate with the advantages of proximity to the conflict and knowledge of (and sometimes leverage with) the parties. However, these strengths can also be these organizations' greatest weakness: they are open to pressure by member states and vulnerable to differences among them.

- Individual states can mediate from positions of relative power and influence over the conflict parties (the United States at Dayton or in the Middle East; and Nigeria, South Africa, Libya, Egypt, India, and Malaysia in their respective regions). Unlike established facilitators, such as Norway and Switzerland—which maintain impartiality regarding the conflicts with which they engage—their own clear interest in a conflict's outcome may be a problem for some parties.

- Private peacemakers are "weak mediators," and so must borrow leverage from others. They can engage early and with discretion with conflict parties that are viewed as pariahs by others or that are reluctant to engage with official actors. Yet the support and cooperation of official actors (states or organizations) will be required to reach and sustain a lasting agreement.

- Prestigious individuals, whether engaged (as with former President Olusegun Obasanjo of Nigeria) as a UN envoy (in the DRC) or working independently, have the advantages of personal stature and extensive prior relationships. Their authority—as seen in the case of Kofi Annan's mediation in Kenya in 2008—can help impose discipline upon the external actors and instill a sense of urgency within the conflict parties.

An assessment of the mediator's capacities, comparative advantages, and comparative disadvantages may help to identify gaps and weaknesses that can be offset by the involvement of individual Friends, or the convening of a group. Does the mediation have broad support within the international community? If the mediation is conducted on behalf of the United Nations, is it in accordance with a mandate of the Security Council, or in the context of the secretary-general's good offices? Does a regional initiative have the relevant regional organization squarely behind it? If it is a bilateral initiative, what are the views of other critical state actors? If a private, or non-governmental, mediator is leading the effort, are key donors or other regional players supportive? If not, is a strategy in place with regard to their involvement at a later date?

In 1999, when Alvaro de Soto assumed the position of special adviser to the UN secretary-general on Cyprus, he found a multitude of special envoys—from Australia, Canada, Finland (this envoy was the EU president at the time), Germany, Russia, Sweden, the United Kingdom, and the United States—already in place. Securing their support was facilitated by the fact that all recognized that a UN-led effort offered the best possible hope for making progress toward settlement of the conflict.

Understand the External Actors

In each conflict, external actors bring different mixes of interests, potential leverage, and logistical and other resources into play. These may be generally positive. If so, coordinating what is being offered in the interests of a coherent strategy becomes the priority. In some instances, however, the external actors may seek to complicate—or even deliberately spoil—the mediation effort, making containment imperative. In yet other cases, they may embrace some combination of the two. The one certainty is that they cannot be ignored.

An international mediator should approach the conflict parties with the understanding that he or she is likely to be perceived as one among the wide variety of external actors engaged. Although the international mediator may have a strong sense of his or her own impartiality, this may not be the perception of the conflict parties—or, indeed, some of the other external actors involved.

Identify Regional Players and Their Interests

Mediators should undertake a rigorous assessment of the interests of neighbors and other regional states in the outcome of a conflict. What are these interests? Security and other interests embracing trade and access to natural resources? Disputed borders? Or concerns directly attributable to the possible consequences of the conflict, including the flow of refugees, arms, and contraband; organized criminal networks; and perhaps even terrorist networks?

Of particular interest will be regional players with a tradition of peacemaking in the region. Even if earlier efforts have not proved to be successful, they may contain elements on which it is possible to build. Have such efforts been undertaken within the context of a regional or subregional organization? If so, how does this organization view the mediator's own initiative? Are there ways in which it may be possible to harness the regional actors' knowledge of and networks within the region? What resources will regional states and organizations be prepared to commit to the peace effort?

The first use of a mechanism specifically identified as Friends of the UN secretary-general was in El Salvador. It was directly related to the regional peace efforts that had preceded the United Nations' engagement as well as the desire of the insurgent Farabundo Mart' Liberation Front (FMLN) to counterbalance the negative influence it feared might be exerted by the United States within the UN Security Council. The group provided the means by which the commitment by Mexico, Colombia, and Venezuela to resolve the conflicts in Central America could be channeled into support for a UN-led peace process. (Spain was added as a fourth Friend on the basis of its active diplomacy in Latin America and the ties it brought to the European Union.)

Immediate neighbors are likely to have direct interests in the conflict in question. This fact suggests that the mediator use caution in engaging them in his or her efforts. At different moments these interests can be usefully employed, but states at least one degree from the conflict theater may prove more tractable partners.

The states bordering on or variously embroiled in regional conflict complexes, such as those centered on the DRC, Sudan, Afghanistan, or the Middle East, present particular challenges. They may supply weapons and political support to repressive states or rebel groups, host them on their territory, extract resources for their own gain, or seek to undermine a peace effort by other means. Building durable regional peace will be slow and difficult. A mediator will need to consider whether it is possible to work toward a comprehensive framework for the settlement of interlocking conflicts, or at least ensure coherent interactions with other negotiation processes within the region.

In 1997, Lakhdar Brahimi, then the UN secretary-general's special adviser for Afghanistan, encouraged the formation of the "six plus two" group of six neighbors—plus the United States and Russia—as a forum in which the possibility of curbing the arms flow into Afghanistan could be raised and regional differences discussed. The initiative did not prosper, and in mid-1999 Brahimi resigned, citing "bitter disappointment" with the six plus two.[4] The experience stood in contrast to the peace process in Tajikistan, where an agreement was reached in 1997, in large part as a consequence of the alignment of the interests of regional actors, gathered in an informal group called Friends of Tajikistan, behind a peaceful settlement of the conflict.

A different set of challenges, but also opportunities, is presented by the big neighbors of states in internal conflict. No durable solution can be found to conflict in the Caucasus that is not at least acceptable to Russia. The same is true of Central America and its big neighbor Mexico, Nepal and Sri Lanka and their big neighbor India, and Somalia and its big neighbor Ethiopia. Mediators must prioritize their contacts with such neighbors, which may have mixed feelings about mediators' engagement in the peace process in the first place, and may eschew the formation of a group of Friends to which a powerful neighbor would be opposed.

In its facilitation of peace talks in Sri Lanka in the early 2000s, Norway prioritized its relationship with India, which led it to decide against the formation of a group of Friends. Key donors—Japan, the European Union, and the United States—were instead involved as co-chairs of a donor mechanism.

Identify Other International Actors

A mediator should also be mindful of the contributions to be made by international actors outside the conflict region. These actors may be powers on the UN Security Council, donors, or others with an interest in and influence over the conflict theater, such as international financial institutions or multinational companies. How and when to engage them may need to be balanced against issues of confidentiality. When possible, however, early and frequent briefings of these potential partners are likely to help build international support for the mediation effort. It may also help overcome the deep-seated divisions found within the Security Council and other multilateral bodies with regard to many cases of complex peacemaking.

Competitive peacemaking, or the appearance of competitive peacemaking, is an unpleasant reality in today's overcrowded mediation field. From Darfur to Nepal to Zimbabwe, mediators have found themselves acting in parallel with, or at cross-currents to, other state, nonstate, and multilateral actors pushing for involvement in the peacemaking effort. With a clearly identified lead often difficult to achieve, mediators need to consider their own relationship to others engaged in peacemaking.

More is not merrier in mediation. The proliferation of rival mediating and facilitation efforts in Burundi during the mid-1990s was a factor in the resignation of Ahmedou Ould Abdallah, the UN secretary-general's special representative. During the Abuja talks on Darfur in 2006, the different messages conveyed to the conflict parties by the external actors helped erode any possibility of a successful outcome.

In order to avoid situations in which parties play rival mediations against one another, a mediator should seek clarity from his or her parent institution, from the conflict parties themselves, and, if possible, from the other mediators or facilitators engaged. The aim should be to develop support for a single negotiating effort and to establish a clear division of roles on the part of external actors, in accordance with their comparative advantages. In the best of circumstances, a group of Friends established in support of an accepted mediator helps to achieve these purposes.

Evaluate Capacities for Leverage and Influence

There are many sources of leverage relevant to a peacemaker.[5] Some sources derive from within the conflict itself, others from internationally supported norms or regimes, and yet others from the mediator's own national or institutional identity, and the political support with which he or she engages. In many circumstances, however, a mediator will look to other external actors to enhance and supplement what he or she is able to bring to the table. Indeed, a principal attraction of a group of Friends is the possibilities it offers of amplifying and diversifying the leverage and influence available to a peacemaking effort.

What this leverage consists of will vary greatly, but is likely to include some mix of diplomatic heavy lifting (perhaps even coercion), assurances with regard to security, and promises of economic resources to come. Mediators should take a hard look at the ability of key external actors to cooperate within a peace process. Without it, the mediation may falter. Do the most significant external actors—in the region, on the UN Security Council, and the major donors—share common purposes in their approach to the conflict? If they are unable to provide consensual support, is the mediation at least tolerated? Will their bilateral priorities allow for the leverage they possess with the conflict parties to be engaged? If the answer to any of these questions is no, then redoubled attention to bilateral diplomacy with the critical external actors will be required in parallel with, or even as a prelude to, their direct engagement with the conflict parties.

A key reason for the intractability of conflicts extending from the Caucasus to Myanmar to Western Sahara is the low priority in their hierarchy of interests that external actors afford conflict resolution there. External actors place a greater premium on relations with Russia, China, India, and Morocco, for example, than they do on pressing forward with policies that might contribute directly to conflict settlement in each case.

Understand Relationships to the Conflict Parties

To help develop a strategy for the engagement of external actors, a mediator should conduct a clear-eyed assessment of external actors' relationships to the conflict parties. Which states—or individuals—have the ears of the conflict parties? Who is supplying arms, engaging in illicit trade, or providing material support of other kinds to the armed actors? Are there economic ties or other connections within the region that can be brought into play? Or are there sources of financing—ranging from international financial institutions to diaspora contributions—that can be linked to progress toward a sustainable peace?

It is often those closest to a given conflict party who are in the best position to encourage flexibility in a negotiation. During the El Salvador negotiations, it was Mexico that put the greatest pressure on the FMLN rebels, and—after an initial period in which the United States viewed the UN-led negotiations with reluctance and skepticism—it was the United States which put the greatest pressure on the Salvadoran government. UN secretariat officials who assembled a Core Group on East Timor included Japan with an eye to the reassurance that its involvement would bring to Indonesia.

What kind of security guarantees will be required to end the conflict? Which institutions or states are the best ones to offer them? Do the conflict parties have an interest in the political dividend that peace might bring? (For example, is a government that can deliver a credible peace deal seeking to command greater legitimacy on the international stage? Is an armed group prepared to sign a peace deal because the group is looking to enhance its credibility both domestically and in the eyes of the international community?)

Mediators must be sensitive to the fact that, in a state-centric international system, most mediations have an overt state bias. Some states that are parties to a conflict may be wary of international involvement because of the legitimacy it could lend to nonstate-armed actors. Others may favor the idea of a group of Friends on the assumption that such Friends will, as representatives of governments and states themselves, naturally be "their" Friends, and so reinforce their hand against insurgents.

At an early stage in the Guatemala talks, President Jorge Serrano sought to put together his own group of Friends. Careful diplomatic footwork by representatives of the states concerned as well as the United Nations was required to walk the initiative backward in order to form a more credible group assembled as Friends of the Guatemalan Peace Process.

Assess the Potential for Collaboration or Spoiler Activities

Although some external actors will offer clear potential as collaborators, others may appear to be potential spoilers. A mediator should try to cultivate relationships with both. With greater familiarity, he or she may be better positioned to fine-tune the collaboration offered and foresee, if not forestall, the spoiler activity.

In considering the potential for collaboration, mediators should seek to encourage unity of effort among the external actors, maximize the influence on and assistance to conflict parties, and build support that will be sustained throughout the implementation of a negotiated settlement and peacebuilding.

Ignoring potential spoilers among the external actors would be risky. A mediator should instead pursue a strategy of containment, usually by rallying support from other international quarters sufficient to weaken and delegitimize the spoiler effort.

Negotiations on Southern Sudan had been complicated for a long time by competing regional peace initiatives. One initiative was led by the Inter-Governmental Authority on Development (IGAD) and was generally favorable to the South's aspirations of self-determination. The other initiative was a joint effort by Egypt and Libya that supported the unity of Sudan. Progress came when support for the IGAD process, led by General Lazaro Sumbeiywo of Kenya, helped contain the rival effort. A critical element was the emergence of an informal Troika of Norway, the United Kingdom, and the United States, which worked to strengthen the IGAD process and keep other potential mediators at bay.

STEP TWO
Develop a Strategy

Working with other external actors in a peace process may prove no less frustrating, time-consuming, or complex than engaging with the conflict parties themselves. A mediator should therefore be prepared to be patient, develop a strategy early, and be open to the need for revisions to it.

The efficacy of a mediator's engagement with external actors will depend to a considerable extent on factors that are difficult to quantify. They include the caliber of his or her leadership and the respect that he or she wins from international colleagues. Engaging early with those who might be helpful in the latter stages of a peace process and/or implementation may encourage their commitment to the effort. Meanwhile, officials' own familiarity with the conflict in question, experience of other peace processes, and overall disposition to work collaboratively will also have an impact. The extent to which these elements are present in a given mediation may boil down to luck.

During 2003, the work of the International Contact Group on Liberia (ICGL) was facilitated by the individual depth of experience and good working rapport between its two co-chairs, Hans Dahlgren, the EU presidency's special representative to the region, and Nana Addo Dunkwa, the foreign minister of Ghana and the chair at the time of the Economic Community of West African States (ECOWAS). They worked together to prepare meetings of the ICGL and conducted joint missions in the region, including meeting with Charles Taylor, then president of Liberia, to impress upon him the need for change.

Weigh the Pros and Cons of a Group Structure

The prevalence of group structures in recent years has made them an attractive—at times, even a default—option. But when the mediator has the opportunity to influence the process, he or she should weigh a group's formation carefully. The potential benefits of grouping the external actors in some way include enhancing the leverage of the mediator, raising the visibility of the peace process, preempting rival mediation initiatives, and preparing for sustained support in implementation. However, groups also have disadvantages.

The question of composition is delicate, as small groups, although undoubtedly more effective, risk excluding—and thus offending—significant potential partners. If a group's members are not like-minded in their approach to a conflict, intergroup dynamics may devolve into complex negotiations of their own. In regionally intertwined conflicts, or conflicts that take place in the shadow of a regional power, what to do about the neighbors will be a constant concern. A strong and cohesive group can overwhelm the mediator and the mediation if its members are not satisfied with the direction taken. A divided one may replicate the differences between the conflict parties, and—even if useful at a procedural level—do little to contribute to the resolution of the conflict.

The Friends of Western Sahara was established on the initiative of the United States in the early 1990s. Its core members—France, Spain, Russia, the United Kingdom, and the United States—were divided on the central issue of self-determination of the Saharawi people, which was championed by the Popular Front for the Liberation of Saguia el Hamra and Rio de Oro (Polisario). And they were driven, to varying degrees, by realpolitik concerns that ensured strong support for Morocco's position that the question of Western Sahara, which Morocco has occupied since 1975, can be resolved only in accordance with its sovereignty and territorial integrity. The group thus managed the issue in the Security Council, but did not prove to be a useful adjunct to the secretary-general's envoys charged with the mediation of the conflict.

Deal with an Existing Group

In a number of long-running conflicts or situations of recurring crisis, appointed UN mediators and other envoys find that a group structure of some kind is already in place. Although such a group can be a source of expertise, contacts, and resources, its prior existence and consolidated identity may place limits upon the mediator's capacity to influence it. Bilateral meetings and consultations with the group's members in advance of and in between encounters with the group as a whole can help the mediator get a clear understanding of the group's internal dynamics and utility as he or she develops a strategy.

Over a period of many years, a mechanism originally formed as the Friends of the Secretary-General for Haiti underwent a number of changes, both in its membership and in its relationship to the UN secretariat. In the latter part of the 1990s, the group was already more frequently referred to as the Friends of Haiti. When the United Nations reengaged in Haiti in 2004, a larger core group was formed in Port-au-Prince, even as the Friends of Haiti drove the decision making in the Security Council.

Although in some circumstances, existing groups experience fundamental changes over the years, in others they have remained similar in structure and purpose. Such groups can present challenges to peacemakers in that their very longevity militates against any sense of urgency. Individual diplomats may join existing groups without any expectation that membership implies anything other than a routine assignment. Friends engaged with a political stalemate may be comfortable with the status quo even as the mediator seeks resolution of the conflict.

In neither the Georgia-Abkhazia nor the Western Sahara conflict did the existing conditions—of cease-fire, refugees, and political acrimony between the parties in contention—directly impinge upon the economic or security interests of most members of the group of Friends. Consequently, they were for many years content to prevent a deterioration of the situation into open hostilities while making little headway in moving matters forward. The brief conflict between Georgia and Russia in August 2008 put to rest the notion of Russia as a "Friend" of Georgia (other members of the Friends—France, Germany, the United Kingdom, and the United States—were informally referred to as the Western Friends)[6] and fundamentally altered the dynamics of the conflict.

Identify an Appropriate Structure

When there is no existing group, a mediator has more room for initiative. However, this room in which to maneuver may be less than at first appears. This is because most Friends, or other structures and coordination mechanisms created to further conflict resolution, are essentially self-selecting, in that their existence is, in the first place, a product of their members' interest in a conflict. The question of a mediator's influence in encouraging or blocking the creation of a group is therefore a sensitive matter, usually involving quiet and careful diplomacy and suggestion.

Before proceeding, a mediator might want to consider first a rough typology of the kinds of structures that have taken shape in the past. These are broadly represented in Table 1. This table, it should be noted, is neither comprehensive nor definitive in its classification of the groups it includes. Indeed, it presents a simplified picture of group structures that have differed widely in their engagement with and impact upon the conflicts concerned, and in some cases have varied in their functions over time.

➤ *Friends of the mediator or process,* whether of the UN secretary-general (as in El Salvador, Georgia, or Haiti) or a specific peace process, are informal structures, generally formed to provide support to peacemaking in contexts in which great power interests are not the driving force. Groups of Friends may be engaged throughout a peace process, although they will fulfill different functions during peacemaking and in helping to implement any subsequent agreement. Related mechanisms may not always carry the name Friends, as the core group formed to support the UN role in East Timor's transition to the independent state of Timor Leste, the Troika in Southern Sudan, and, indeed, the very different core groups engaged in implementation in Cambodia and Mozambique and supporting negotiations in Northern Uganda all illustrate.

➤ *An ad hoc arrangement* (the "no group" option) has been preferred by mediators for various reasons. These include questions of expediency in situations in which mediations have been conducted under tight time pressure (as in Kenya in 2008), but also concerns that the identification of a closed group of Friends might be counterproductive. The formation of an identifiable group structure might be rejected because it would

Table 1. Major Groups of Friends and Related Mechanisms, 1990–2009

	Friends of the Mediator or Process	Ad Hoc Arrangements	Contact Groups	Implementation or Monitoring Groups	Assistance Coordination Mechanisms
Afghanistan		No group preferred after Bonn Agreement, 2001–05	Six Plus Two, 1997–2001		Afghan Support Group, 1997–2002; Af-Pak Support Group, 2009–
Angola	Friends of Angola, 1999–2002		Troika, 1990–2002	Joint Commission, 1994–2002	
Bolivia	OAS Friends of Bolivia, 2008				
Burundi	NGO Friends, 1994–95	Regional Peace Initiative, 1995–2009		International Monitoring Commission, 2000–05; Partnership for Peace, 2009–	ECOSOC Ad Hoc Advisory Group, 2003–06; Partners Coordination Group, 2008–
Cambodia	Core Group, 2002–03				
Colombia	Friends of Government–ELN talks, 2000–2003, 2005–; Friends of Government–FARC talks, 2001–02				

continued

Table 1. Major Groups of Friends and Related Mechanisms, 1990–2009 (continued)

	Friends of the Mediator or Process	Ad Hoc Arrangements	Contact Groups	Implementation or Monitoring Groups	Assistance Coordination Mechanisms
Cyprus		Unidentified Friends of the UN Secretary-General, 1999–2003			
DRC				CIAT 2002–06 Joint Monitoring Group, 2007–	Contact Group, 2004–
Côte d'Ivoire		International Working Group, 2005–07	ECOWAS Contact Group, 2004–05	Monitoring Group, 2005–07	
East Timor	Core Group, 1999–		Support Group, 1999		
El Salvador	Friends of UN Secretary-General for El Salvador, 1990–97				
Ethiopia/Eritrea				Friends of UNMEE, 2000–08	
Former Yugoslavia			Contact Group, 1994–		

Step 2: Develop a Strategy

	Friends of the Mediator or Process	Ad Hoc Arrangements	Contact Groups	Implementation or Monitoring Groups	Assistance Coordination Mechanisms
Georgia	Friends of Georgia/ of UN Secretary-General for Georgia, 1993–2008				
Guatemala	Friends of the Guatemalan Peace Process, 1993–2004				Dialogue Group, 2000–2006
Guinea–Bissau			International Contact Group, 2006–		Friends of Guinea Bissau, 1999–2008; ECOSOC Ad Hoc Advisory Group, 2002–08
Haiti	Friends of the UN Secretary-General for Haiti 1992–2001; OAS Friends of Haiti, 2001–; (UN) Friends of Haiti, 2004–				Core Group on Haiti, 2004–; ECOSOC Ad Hoc Advisory Group, 2004–
	OAS Dialogue Group, 2009				

continued

29

Table 1. Major Groups of Friends and Related Mechanisms, 1990–2009 (continued)

	Friends of the Mediator or Process	Ad Hoc Arrangements	Contact Groups	Implementation or Monitoring Groups	Assistance Coordination Mechanisms
Indonesia/ Aceh	Centre for Humanitarian Dialogue's "Wise Men" and Friends or "Group of Four," 2001–03				
Lebanon					Core Group, 2005–08
Liberia			International Contact Group I, 1995–96; International Contact Group II, 2002–07	International Monitoring Commission, 2004–06	
Madagascar			International Contact Group, 2009–		
Mauritania			International Contact Group, 2008–		
Middle East			Quartet, 2001–		
Mozambique	Core Group, 2002–04				

	Friends of the Mediator or Process	Ad Hoc Arrangements	Contact Groups	Implementation or Monitoring Groups	Assistance Coordination Mechanisms
Myanmar	Friends of the UN Secretary-General for Myanmar, 2008–	Informal Consultation Group, 1994–2007			
Nagorno-Karabakh			Minsk Group, 1992–		
Namibia			Western Contact Group, 1977–90	Joint Monitoring Committee, 1988–90	
Pakistan					Friends of Democratic Pakistan, 2008–
Philippines			International Contact Group, 2009–		
Sierra Leone			International Contact Group, 1998–99		

continued

Table 1. Major Groups of Friends and Related Mechanisms, 1990–2009 (continued)

	Friends of the Mediator or Process	Ad Hoc Arrangements	Contact Groups	Implementation or Monitoring Groups	Assistance Coordination Mechanisms
Somalia			Contact Group/ External Actors, 1998–2007 International Contact Group, 2006–		
Sri Lanka					Co-chairs donor mechanism, 2002–09
Sudan	IPF Core Group, 1995– Troika, 1999–2004		Contact Group, 2005–	Assessment and Evaluation Commission, 2004–	
Tajikistan	Friends of Tajikistan, 1995–96		Contact Group, 1997–2000		
Uganda	Core Group/ Group of 7 plus 1, 2004–08				
Venezuela	OAS Friends of Venezuela, 2004–05				
Western Sahara	Friends of Western Sahara, 1992–				

exclude regional or other critical actors, which would not be positioned to play a constructive role; or it might be rejected because key states—such as a powerful neighbor—demonstrate a clear preference for bilateral consultations; or it might be rejected simply because a given mediator prefers the greater flexibility of a more ad hoc approach.

In Cyprus, UN envoys have traditionally maintained particularly close relationships with both the United Kingdom and the United States in their interactions with the Cypriot parties, Greece, and Turkey. During the course of the effort undertaken between 1999 and 2004, Secretary-General Kofi Annan publicly expressed his gratitude for the support of states he recognized as "Friends." However, he never identified who these Friends were, out of deference to the various degrees of support his effort received from other interested states and actors, such as the European Union.

During the Bonn negotiations on Afghanistan in 2001 and subsequent to them, the UN mediator Lakhdar Brahimi worked closely with a variety of regional and more distant states. However, both numbers and divergent interests—particularly among the regional actors—militated against the formation of a group of Friends. More flexible forms of consultation were instead pursued.

➤ *Contact groups* are groups of the major powers interested in the outcome of a conflict. They have been vehicles for these powers' direct diplomacy in a variety of different peace processes, representing both powerful partners and—at times—major headaches for the mediators. Since the days of the Contact Group on Namibia (the first example of its kind, this group crafted the plan that became the basis for the Namibia settlement), big power contact groups have been self-selecting. Reaching an agreement among members of such a group will generally be a necessary prerequisite to moving toward a solution of the conflict, but this is unlikely to fall within the competencies of an outside mediator.

The Contact Group on the former Yugoslavia was created in 1994, in part to circumvent the United Nations. Since then, it has allowed for differences among the states with the most obvious interests in regional stability to be hammered out away from the glare of Security Council attention. The protracted discussions about the final status of Kosovo demonstrated that the ability of even a very senior UN envoy (Ahtisaari) to mediate among the group's members was limited.

Larger and more flexible contact groups created in Africa to harness regional expertise and outside resources have maintained a variety of relationships to the mediations concerned. They have generally focused on issues of coordination, oversight, and fundraising, rather than operational aspects of peacemaking, but have become increasingly prevalent as a means of addressing emerging conflicts or situations of political crisis.

- *A continuing tendency to create contact groups in Africa was illustrated in 2008–2009, when the African Union (AU) responded to successive crises in Mauritania, Guinea, and Madagascar with the creation of a contact group for each state. Each group was composed of the five permanent and elected African members of the Security Council, and representatives of the regional and international organizations to which the particular state belonged.*

- *Implementation and monitoring groups* are distinguished by a mandate establishing their responsibilities in a peace agreement, and thus are a direct product of negotiations. They have varied greatly in the extent to which they are directly engaged in monitoring activities. In some circumstances, mechanisms have followed the model established in Namibia, where a Joint Monitoring Commission was chaired by the representative of the UN secretary-general and included representatives of the parties to the conflict as well as key external actors. In other situations, such as the DRC, where an International Commission to Accompany the Transition (CIAT) was established in the peace agreement, they did not include the conflict parties.

   During its existence, which ran from the signing of the peace agreement in late 2002 until elections held at the end of 2006, the CIAT developed a degree of affinity to a Friends' group in the functions it fulfilled. Convened by the special representative of the UN secretary-general, it undertook mediation tasks and published regular communiqués that sought to maintain pressure on the Congolese parties to abide by their commitments under the peace agreement.

- *Assistance coordination mechanisms* beyond the parameters of the monitoring of an agreement have also proliferated, with varying relationships to the mediation or political efforts that are still in place. The Ad Hoc Liaison Committee for Assistance to the Palestinian People was created to support the Oslo Peace Accords; the Peace Implementation Council in Bosnia brought together a large number of actors to oversee assistance and decision making after the Dayton agreements. The co-chaired group of donors for Sri Lanka was more modest in scope. This group was established at a moment at which—too optimistically, as it turned out—coordination of assistance for an advancing peace process seemed to be the priority. Different again was the Friends of Democratic Pakistan group, which in 2008 and 2009 sought to promote coherence in international support for Pakistan as it faced protracted political and security challenges.

The Case of the Private Peacemaker

Private, or nongovernmental, peacemakers have no political or economic weight of their own and thus bring neither direct leverage nor the promise of resources to the negotiating table. Although the discretion and flexibility with which they are able to engage may make them the mediators of choice in some circumstances—particularly in the early stages of a peace process or in establishing contacts with armed groups with which states prefer not to engage—their success depends on leverage that is borrowed from others.

This was demonstrated in the negotiations on Mozambique, when the Community of Sant'Egidio sought support from international observers. These observers later came to form a core group that worked with the United Nations to implement the resulting peace agreement. Meanwhile, in an early period of peace talks on Aceh, Indonesia, the Centre for Humanitarian Dialogue established both a group of "Wise Men," which, although composed of individuals, implicitly brought with it the engagement of significant states, and more distant "Friends" that lent their weight on key issues.

Private peacemakers of great renown can use their personal prestige to good effect, both with the conflict parties and in securing support from other external actors. This was demonstrated by the successful effort on Aceh led by Martti Ahtisaari in the wake of the December 2004 tsunami. The conflict parties were impressed by his status as a former president, and his private mediation was able to pave the way for a monitoring mechanism established by the European Union, Norway, Switzerland, and five contributing countries from the Association of Southeast Asian Nations (ASEAN).

Although an all-NGO group of Friends was briefly constituted in Burundi in the mid-1990s, the International Contact Group on the Southern Philippines formed in late 2009 represented an interesting innovation: a mixed membership of states (Japan, Turkey, and the United Kingdom) and nongovernmental organizations (the Centre for Humanitarian Dialogue, which also served as the group's coordinator; the Asia Foundation; Conciliation Resources; and Muhammadiyah).

Choose Friends with Care

In the (relatively few) circumstances in which a mediator has the luxury of choosing his or her Friends, they should be chosen with great care and with close attention to what each will bring to the process. The mediator should remember that it is the support that can be offered to the peace effort, rather than the existence of a group structure, that is the priority. With this in mind, the mediator may want to consider a strategy that involves informal coalitions instead of a group of Friends or a strategy that allows for time spent testing potential Friends in separate and noncommittal meetings before a group is constituted.

In both El Salvador and East Timor, groups of states that had the appearance of emerging organically were carefully nurtured by the UN officials involved. A cautious approach ("pre-cooking") ensured that the mediators knew their interlocutors well before either group took shape.

Most successful groups of Friends have been small in number (four to six states). However, many states are likely to press for inclusion within a Friends group—regardless of whether or not they have much to offer it. Consequently, a mediator will want to pay attention to the delicate question of gatekeeping.

In the late 1990s, states pushed for inclusion in both a group of Friends of Angola and an Informal Consultation Group on Myanmar. Both groups were created at the United Nations, with the Myanmar group limited to support of the secretary-general's effort to fulfill the human rights and democratization mandate given to him by the General Assembly. The group's expanded size led to structures that, while useful for the purposes of information sharing, were too unwieldy for flexible and collaborative engagement. (On his assumption of responsibilities for Angola in early 2000, Ibrahim Gambari, Annan's special adviser on Africa, was able to reduce the size of the Friends of Angola from around twenty to a more manageable—if still sizable—eleven.) The desire to become involved in these and other mechanisms reflects the curious fact that, in the public sphere at least, states have little to lose from participation as a "Friend," as the appearance of making a contribution to a group (even an ineffective one) may be almost as relevant as actually doing so.

Assess Individual Friends' Potential Contribution

What a group is expected to do is an essential element of its formation. In circumstances in which the mediator has direct control or more discreet influence over the formation of a group, efforts should be made to ensure that its membership is results oriented. A mediator must consider who brings what to the table. Will external actors be prepared to follow the mediator's lead? Will they remain open to the possibility of developing complementary initiatives or be ready and able to make a substantial contribution to the peacemaking effort? What this contribution might involve will vary. It is likely, however, to include some combination of logistical, substantive, and financial support to the mediation itself; assistance to, encouragement of, or pressure on one or more of the conflict parties; public support of the process and any resulting agreement in order to build credibility and enhance legitimacy; and economic and perhaps even security guarantees for the implementation process.

Although a mediator may choose Friends with a view to their potential utility as partners in implementation, a lack of financial or material resources on the part of a regional or other actor should not preclude the actor's involvement. This is particularly true of an actor that has political leverage over one or more parties to the conflict. Nor should membership on the Security Council, whether permanent or temporary, be taken as a determining criterion for membership in a group. However, the inclusion of states with an overriding strategic interest in the outcome of a particular conflict, or a proxy relationship with one of the parties, would have inevitable consequence for the engagement of a Friends' group and should generally be avoided.

Efforts to form a Committee of Friends of Somalia in 2002 fell apart as states from the region, widely considered more "enemy" than "friend" by many Somalis, pressed for inclusion. Meanwhile, the big powers on the Security Council, haunted by the events of the early 1990s, were unsure about how to engage with a country lacking a recognized government and stayed well clear of any heavy lifting. Renewed attention to Somalia in mid-2006 saw the creation of a new International Contact Group on Somalia, in part as an expression of a shift in U.S. policy after Islamists won control of Mogadishu from U.S.-backed militias.

In addition to questions of size, mediators should consider the extent to which potential groups of Friends reflect sufficient commonality of interests among their members. Mediators should also reflect on whether there is an acceptable balance among big powers, which are likely to pursue their national and global priorities within the narrow confines of a group; regional actors; and well-intentioned "helpful-fixer" states with less at stake but also less real leverage over the conflict parties. The interests may be diverse, but experience suggests that Friends should hold in common an overriding interest in a peaceful settlement of conflict and a shared sense of what that might look like.

In situations in which individual Friends had a greater interest in the stability or continuing existence of one or the other parties to a conflict than in the conflict's resolution—as was the case in both Georgia and Western Sahara—the usefulness of the Friends as a means to move toward a settlement suffered. Meanwhile, regional actors—such as Mexico in Central America, Australia and New Zealand in East Timor, and Ghana in West Africa—with direct interests in the peace and security at stake, have been motivated to play a leading role within the group structure formed to address conflicts in their own neighborhood.

Assess Optimum Timing for the Initiative

There can be no fixed rules for the timing of a Friends initiative. Friends and other groups fill distinct but interrelated roles during peacemaking, in implementation of a subsequent agreement, and in support of peacebuilding. Although what such groups can offer will vary at different stages of a process, they are most productive when they have a process to support, or a clearly assigned job to do. It is with a clear sense of what this job will be, and how the Friends will support it, that a mediator should consider their formation.

A mediator should be wary of forming a group of Friends simply because he or she cannot think of anything else to do. In the absence of the political will to move forward on the part of the conflict parties, Friends on their own cannot unblock a stalemate or push through a peace settlement. Moreover, the mere fact of participation within a group may not help external actors that are starkly divided in their approaches to a conflict overcome their differences.

At various moments, UN officials considered the elevation of the Informal Consultation Group on Myanmar into a group of Friends as a means of furthering a coherent international approach to the country. The idea was rejected in 2006, but a group of Friends of the Secretary-General for Myanmar was eventually formed in 2007. It did little to bridge the gulf between the resistance in the region to the idea of external intervention—encouraged by trade and other issues binding China, India, and Thailand to their problematic neighbor—and Western states' concern to exact concessions from the country's authoritarian rulers.

But with patience and under certain circumstances, external actors can play a role in moving parties toward substantive negotiations. Parties to a conflict may at first be reluctant to countenance the appearance of international intervention represented by a group mechanism. Yet a mediator who has a clear sense that there are benefits to be gained from Friends should expend time and effort in explaining these to the conflict parties. Increased interaction with the Friends themselves may also help assuage such doubts. In a best-case scenario, the "ripening" of a conflict for negotiation may occur in parallel with the emergence of an obvious group of Friends.

Knowledge of the parties involved and a deep commitment to an eventual peace could be seen in the efforts of Spain, Mexico, and Norway to nurture a fragile peace process in Guatemala from its earliest days. Once UN-moderated negotiations took shape, the accompaniment provided by these international actors, acting independently, and then configured as Friends (alongside the United States, Colombia, and Venezuela) provided an essential continuity to the process.

A further consideration regarding the timing of the creation of the group is the bilateral positions of the states concerned. These may shift in accordance with the vicissitudes of the conflict itself or with a change in their policies toward it.

For many years, Francesc Vendrell, a senior UN official engaged in the talks between Indonesia and Portugal on East Timor, resisted suggestions to recommend the formation of a group of Friends. He feared that powerful states' support of Indonesia would cause any group formed to exert pressure on Portugal to let East Timor go. In 1999, however, when a change in policy by Indonesia opened up the possibility of the Timorese achieving self-determination, he recommended that the secretary-general form a core group analogous to a group of Friends.

STEP THREE
Engage with Friends and Conflict Parties

The extent to which a mediator is able to encourage Friends' direct engagement with the conflict parties will vary from conflict to conflict. In the interests of keeping the process confidential and maintaining focus, it may not be advisable to have them at the negotiating table—and certainly not at all times. However, a mediator should seek other means to ensure their diplomatic and material support for the process. Direct involvement in peacemaking brings benefits in the short term. It also may help solidify a Friend's commitment for the long haul of implementation and peacebuilding that will follow a successful mediation.

Seek Support for Mediation Role

Maintaining leadership during a mediation process is a subtle art. One important reason is that this "leadership" is of coure subordinated to positions taken by the conflict parties themselves. These factions will have to make the decisions and implement the agreements necessary to move the conflict forward toward a sustainable peace. Only significant time invested by mediators in cultivating partnerships among Friends and other actors will allow for the development of the trust, respect, and perhaps even a degree of complicity (sometimes employed with respect to each official's parent bureaucracy) required to sustain support and to forestall the appearance of rival initiatives.

As the secretary-general's personal representative charged with the mediation of the negotiations on El Salvador, Alvaro de Soto cultivated an impresarial relationship with the Friends. He would describe himself as the "very authoritarian conductor" of a quintet whose other members were the four Friends.[7] This led to a certain amount of grumbling on their part, although the Friends were broadly appreciative of the discretion and skill with which he and UN Secretary-General Javier Pérez de Cuéllar worked with them and the conflict parties.

The establishment of a peace operation under the authority of a special representative of the secretary-general (SRSG) in theory introduces a degree of clarity to the question of leadership. In practice, however, SRSGs themselves command widely varying degrees of influence, according to the different political contexts, mandates, and personalities involved.

UN processes in which a permanent member of the Security Council believes its interests are directly at stake are particularly complex, even when a Friends' group is involved. In Haiti, Georgia, and Western Sahara, for example, the strong grip on the diplomatic process maintained by (respectively) the United States, Russia, and France ensured that the bottom line was not subject to "leadership" from the secretariat. The political direction of international engagement in the Balkans was consistently determined by the politics of the Contact Group, rather than the "leadership" of a UN or other envoy.

Seek Logistical, Financial, and Military Assistance

Friends can provide a mediator with a variety of forms of support and assistance. Most obviously, they can be called upon for logistical and financial support to facilitate the preparation and holding of negotiations. This can include direct support for the mediation itself (covering travel and staffing costs) as well as the hosting of meetings with and between the parties. These are most likely to take place outside the conflict theater, for reasons of both security and discretion. Whether they take place in a Friend country or elsewhere will depend on a variety of political and geographic considerations.

A mediator may need to enlist the assistance of Friends, or at least friendly states, in facilitating the travel of representatives of nonstate-armed groups. If they must cross an international border, they are likely to require assistance with passports and visas, and perhaps also security guarantees, which only an outside third party would be able to provide.

During the El Salvador negotiations, individual representatives of the Friends escorted FMLN leaders whenever they left rebel-held territory for negotiations outside the country. Over the years, Norway and Switzerland—neither of which is a member of the European Union and thus are not bound by its strictures with respect to listed terrorists—have separately facilitated discreet meetings with a variety of nonstate-armed groups.

The extent to which Friends are willing and able to provide military assistance, including peacekeepers, will vary greatly. Indeed, patterns of troop contribution at the United Nations reflect an increasing divergence between the powerful and well-resourced states most frequently engaged as Friends, which pay many of the bills for peacekeeping through assessed contributions, and those which provide it with troops. (The majority of troops contributed to UN peace operations are from the global south, with the five largest contributors as of November 2009, for example, being Pakistan, Bangladesh, India, Nigeria, and Egypt.) However, mediators should encourage Friends with a strong political/regional or other interest in a peace operation to make substantial troop commitments, as these have been seen to have positive results for the coherence and capacities of peace operations.

Since its establishment in 2004, the United Nations Stabilization Mission in Haiti (MINUSTAH) has benefited from the unprecedented contribution by Latin American states, with Brazil at the forefront. Over time, a direct correlation between the contribution of troops to the mission and membership in the Friends has developed. Troop contributors were invited to join the Friends in New York and the largest among them maintained considerable influence over decisions made by the Security Council.

Explore Enhanced Access to Information and Substantive Expertise

Mediators will benefit from the varied networks and access to information that Friends can offer. In some cases, this may extend to information gleaned from intelligence networks that most mediators are unlikely to have at their disposal.

Mediators may also call upon Friends to provide or support substantive expertise required for the mediation. In certain cases, Friends might support or finance individual experts to work as part of the mediator's team for the duration of the peacemaking. In others, Friends might ensure that experts on issues such as power sharing or wealth sharing, transitional justice, or security-sector reform are brought in to support the mediation or even work with the conflict parties directly.

In Southern Sudan, the Troika helped to ensure that the IGAD mediation received the technical and other expertise it required, including a Norwegian expert on wealth sharing. Switzerland has prioritized the provision of technical expertise to a wide variety of peace processes (including Southern Sudan, Uganda, and Nepal), whether it is formally involved in a group mechanism or not.

A recent development is the availability of flexible standby assistance through the UN mediation support unit.[8] Funded by Norway, this initiative builds on Norway's experience as a facilitator and Friend. Standby assistance exemplifies the benefits that mediators can gain from rapidly deployable expertise.

Involve Friends in Building Credibility

Mediators should seek support from Friends in building the credibility of the peace process, both with domestic constituencies directly affected by the conflict—whom may have little confidence in the will or ability of the conflict parties to move toward peace—and with the international community. Careful coordination of public messages of support for the process from Friends and the direct involvement of Friends as witnesses to an agreement can contribute toward this goal.

In Guatemala, the involvement of the Friends enhanced the credibility of the peace process with the sectors opposed to a negotiated settlement. If states such as Mexico, Spain, and the United States supported it, the peace process could not be all bad. It also helped create what UN moderator Jean Arnault would later describe as "a framework of parity, in which both parties believe they can negotiate without losing status."[9]

The question of credibility extends to the mediator as well. Mediators should encourage Friends to reassure state parties that they will not be asked to do anything considered unreasonable from the perspective of governments with which they may have long-established relationships. Under such circumstances, such Friends can assuage doubts that the state party may hold regarding the partiality of the mediator toward nonstate actors (a common problem).

Meanwhile, an individual representative of a Friend state with deep knowledge of a conflict can be a useful advocate within his or her own government for a peace process. He or she is likely to know more about the conflict in question than any other individual within his or her government and should become a reference point for national positions and initiatives.

During the negotiations on Southern Sudan, the British government created a Sudan Unit, which was jointly staffed by the Foreign and Commonwealth Office and the Department for International Development. The unit was headed by Alan Goulty, the United Kingdom's special envoy to Sudan and a driving force within the Troika.

Develop Friends' Engagement with Conflict Parties

As representatives of states, Friends are likely to have existing relationships with state parties to a conflict. Yet the extent to which they will have prior knowledge and experience of nonstate conflict parties will vary greatly. This, as well as their own positions on the demands and practices of the nonstate actors (possibly extending to their listing as a terrorist organization, either bilaterally or by a multilateral organization of which the Friend may be a member), will affect their ability to work with them within a peace process.

Acknowledge State/Nonstate Actor Sensitivities

Mediators must be sensitive to the pro-state bias of most peace processes as they consider how Friends may most helpfully reinforce their efforts with the conflict parties.

A state in conflict, under threat from one or more insurgencies or secessionist movements, is likely to see itself as an upstanding member of the international community, besieged by actors it holds as delinquent, criminal, or terrorist. It therefore may expect states involved as Friends to hold a similar bias.

Officials in Tbilisi welcomed the involvement of the Western members of the Friends, whose clear rejection of the aspirations of Abkhazia's secessionist forces undermined any prospect of impartiality. Meanwhile, in the absence of a third-party mediator, the Colombian government assumed that ambassadors involved in the Friends mechanism during talks with the

Revolutionary Armed Forces of Colombia in 2002 would be agents of its own interest in defeating a terrorist group with well-documented involvement in the illicit drug trade.

A government may grudgingly come to accept the need for a mediator to exercise impartiality toward the conflict parties. But the implicit recognition of the legitimacy of nonstate actors by other states will be more problematic. Governments can therefore view a Friend's efforts to reach out to nonstate-armed actors with suspicion.

Some representatives of the states (Norway, Spain, and Switzerland) involved in Colombia as Friends of the peace process with the National Liberation Army (ELN) were criticized by the government for demonstrating partiality toward terrorist groups.

An additional factor complicating the development of parity at the negotiating table is the question of access to multilateral forums in which the conflict might be discussed, particularly the United Nations. State parties to conflict can address such forums directly; nonstate parties cannot. Although some nonstate parties have benefited from liaison offices in New York and elsewhere (among them the FMLN, the Guatemalan National Revolutionary Unity [URNG], and Polisario), they, like other conflict parties, such as the Abkhaz or Kosovar Albanians, clearly labor at a diplomatic disadvantage relative to their state opponents.[10]

Sometimes the direct engagement of Friends with nonstate actors will develop naturally from a familiarity with the nonstate actors and their goals. Other times this will not be the case, and mediators will need to assess how useful it would be to pursue this engagement. In many circumstances, pro-state inclinations among Friends will complicate their engagement and even undermine the utility of Friends as intermediaries.

More positively, mediators should recognize the potential of Friends in situations involving well-established nonstate-armed actors with effective leadership, control of territory, or a defined political agenda. When nonstate actors seek their own strategy for diplomatic engagement, external actors offer particularly promising entry points.

The initial impetus to form a group mechanism in El Salvador came from the FMLN. Its negotiators were wary of the influence of the United States in the Security Council and sought a way to counter it. In this they had common cause with the UN secretary-general, whose own capacity for independent action in the backyard of the United States was limited by the politics of the Cold War.

The more positive cases of engagement with Friends have occurred when elements of the demands of the nonstate parties have been broadly acceptable to the international community. In several instances, these demands (for justice; for respect for human, economic, and social rights; and so on) have been, at least in part, legitimized by practices—such as flouting the rule of law and violating human rights—adopted by the state actors involved (not that the nonstate actors were blameless in this regard). In several cases, these positive examples also reflect a history of engagement with external actors that helped sensitize nonstate and international actors to each other's expectations.

In Southern Sudan, John Garang's Sudan People's Liberation Movement/ Army (SPLM/A) pursued sophisticated interactions with the international community. This was facilitated by the behavior of the government of Sudan and laid the basis for the effective role played by the international community in support of the process that concluded in the Comprehensive Peace Agreement (CPA). In situations in Angola and Colombia, in contrast, well-resourced nonstate actors showed little inclination to engage with the outside world and still less to modify human rights or other practices, making it easy for self-styled "Friends" to dismiss them as criminal.

Engage Leverage Where Appropriate

The involvement of a variety of states within a Friends group brings with it the possibility of different kinds of leverage, in accordance with their differing interests and capacities. The mediator can work with the Friends group to ensure coordination among members in pulling different "levers" at distinct stages of the process.

A mediator may wish to ask a Friend, or potential Friend, to help build the capacity of conflict parties—through bilateral engagement, workshops, or other activities—in advance of any attempt to bring the parties together. Friends can be informal channels to the conflict parties, reinforcing the positions and views assumed by the mediator, and assisting him or her in building support for the parties' own negotiators, who are likely to face an array of pressures from their own constituencies. The greater the familiarity of the Friends group with the conflict parties, the greater the capacity of the group to exert leverage upon the conflict parties at critical moments in the peace process.

As a Friend of the Guatemalan peace process, Norway provided direct support to the URNG to facilitate its participation in negotiations. At later stages, it conducted a series of meetings and workshops with individuals within the Guatemalan military in an effort to build their confidence in the peace process. During negotiations in Oslo in 1995, Norwegian officials successfully used their knowledge of the parties to exert pressure on them to agree to a Historical Clarification Commission.

As a mediation progresses and relationships of mutual trust develop between the mediator and the Friends—as well as among them—natural divisions of labor may emerge, allowing for the different actors involved to calibrate their interactions with the parties.

In an effective division of labor within the Troika in Sudan, the United States was more overtly favorable to the south and the United Kingdom to the government of Sudan. Norway fell somewhere in between. In their interventions, the three were helped by their representatives' deep knowledge of Sudan and familiarity with many of the Sudanese actors involved. Successive UN mediators on Cyprus, meanwhile, drew on the United Kingdom's deep ties to Greece and the United States' leverage with both Greece and Turkey as they sought to harness regional support for negotiations between the Cypriot communities' leaders.

Mediators can call upon Friends to deliver a message to conflict parties or to influence them. This message might be transmitted through a well-timed telephone call or at a meeting conducted at one degree from the mediation itself. Friends can offer encouragement and reassurance to a conflict party regarding the steps it should take and, at times, spell out the negative consequences (in terms of security or economic or other assistance) likely to transpire if the desired action is not taken. Sometimes such a message is best delivered by a specific Friend with influence over the party concerned. At other times, repeated iterations of the same message from different Friends will be most effective. And at yet other times, the message may carry more weight if delivered by a joint delegation of Friends.

Step 3: Engage with Friends and Conflict Parties

It is no coincidence that almost all groups of Friends have counted the United States among their members. Although the United States need not be in the lead of a Friend effort, U.S. support, including its leverage at critical moments, has proved vital in securing agreement in cases as varied as East Timor, Guatemala, and Southern Sudan. In the exceptional case of El Salvador, where the United States was not a Friend, its support of the negotiations in their final stages, in partnership with the Friends group, was a critical factor in their successful conclusion. During implementation, the United States joined the Friends in a formula that became known as the "four plus one."

STEP FOUR
Sustain Coordinated Support

For a mediator, the possibility of sustained coordinated support for a peace process is one of the primary attractions of a Friends mechanism. The first locus of this coordination will be the ambassadors or special envoys with whom the mediator interacts on the most frequent basis (in the conflict theater or, for a UN envoy, sometimes in New York). However, a particular advantage offered by Friends is that, as representatives of states rather than individuals, they may be simultaneously available to the mediator in a variety of locations and at a variety of levels within each government.

In the best of circumstances, this allows the mediator to encourage the coherence with which each Friend state engages with a conflict situation and/or mediation. This will be facilitated in situations in which Friend states designate an individual to coordinate their efforts on a particular conflict. For a mediator who is accustomed to contending with (or being confused by) policies fragmented within and across different government departments and agencies, this can be an asset.

Mediators should also seek to work with Friends to develop coordinated support within regional and multilateral organizations. This can be particularly helpful for mediations that appear to be progressing toward agreements that call for peace operations to monitor and support their implementation.

IGAD's mediation on Southern Sudan benefited from the links to the broader international community provided by the Troika as well as the presence of the United Nations—which had no formal political role on Sudan—as an observer to the talks. These arrangements helped prepare the UN Security Council for the creation of a UN peacekeeping operation to monitor implementation of the CPA.

Try to Maintain Consensus within the Friends

Friends will not agree on every aspect of a peace process, but the maintenance of a broad consensus on its direction and goals will be central to their utility. Peacemakers may need to exhibit patience and persistence to encourage this consensus to take shape and then hold.

Encourage a "Like-minded" Approach

Minor differences between the peacemaker and individual Friends, or, indeed, the Friends as a collective, are an inevitable—and probably healthy—part of the fabric of a complex negotiation. But they should not threaten the commonality in approach to the peace process upon which the engagement of the peacemaker and the Friend is based.

A mediator should understand that the outcome of self-sustaining peace and stability, toward which he or she is working, would have both explicit and implicit benefits for the Friends. This will be harder to keep in mind if the parties are locked in a zero-sum approach toward issues such as self-determination or secession, particularly if some of the positions within the Friends reinforce those of the conflict parties themselves. Other complex environments include those in which the perceived optimum outcome for many in the international community is the military defeat of one of the conflict parties.

Differences within the co-chair mechanism on Sri Lanka were rooted in the various attitudes of its members toward engagement with the Liberation Tigers of Tamil Eelam (LTTE), a group justifiably criticized for its terrorist practices but whose existence nevertheless reflected deep inequities within the Sri Lankan state.

A mediator can seek to adopt a variety of strategies with the Friends. These might include encouraging them to work with the conflict parties on modest but achievable goals—such as humanitarian access, technical support, human rights monitoring, or even modalities for a cease-fire—while avoiding, or at least delaying, addressing the core issues that divide them. At times, it may be necessary to propose initiatives whose primary purpose is to energize the Friends or preserve unity among them.

In early 2003, UN officials attempted to counter an impasse that had developed within the Friends of Georgia between Russia and the group's

Western members by initiating a new process, the "Geneva process," to facilitate discussion of substantive issues without casting to one side—as Russia would have preferred—the contentious question of Abkhazia's political status. Although successful in that the process created the appearance of movement, the initiative could not counter the underlying differences among the Friends or deep distrust between the parties.

Differences among the external actors will be exploited by conflict parties, which will, quite naturally, be trying to gain maximum advantage from any such fissures. Conflict parties may be encouraged by one or more of their interlocutors to believe that it would serve them well to hold out for a better deal.

The incoherence of the international effort on Darfur during the Abuja talks of 2006 stood in marked contrast to support provided during the negotiation of the CPA on Southern Sudan. The negotiations were attended not only by the African Union but also, at various times, by representatives of the United Nations and the European Union, Nigeria, Chad, Libya, and Eritrea (the latter three with pronounced interests of their own at stake), as well as a variety of representatives of the United States, the United Kingdom, Canada, France, the Netherlands, and Norway. Managing their competing levels of interest and engagement proved beyond the scope of the AU mediation. The conflict parties received a variety of messages from these disparate international partners that directly encouraged their intransigence.

Forestall Unilateral Initiatives

Membership in a group of Friends implies at least tacit agreement to a consolidated effort toward peace. This may range from an overt commitment to work in support of the mediator and take only initiatives that have been suggested, requested, or at least cleared by him or her, to a looser arrangement in which cohesion within the Friends—and commitment to the peace process—is used to reinforce a weaker mediator. In both situations, good faith and solidarity on the part of the group of Friends should prevent the launching of unilateral initiatives by individual Friends.

During the talks on Cyprus that took place in the early years of this century, the United Kingdom and the United States were specifically asked by UN Secretary-General Kofi Annan to "respect the UN's impartiality and independence and . . . accept at every stage that the UN was in the lead."[11]

There are, however, circumstances in which an individual Friend that has privileged access to one or more of the conflict parties may feel frustrated by the course taken by the mediator or the slow development of the peace process and thus feel tempted to go it alone. The mediator will, of course, soon learn of the initiative and should take steps either to "own" the initiative, if it strikes him or her as a positive one, or to distance himself or herself from it and attempt to persuade the errant Friend to maintain a disciplined approach.

In July 1991, at a moment at which the Salvadoran talks were stalled on the future of the armed forces, the Venezuelan president, Carlos Andrés Pérez, summoned the conflict parties to Caracas and tried to persuade them to sign an agreement, presented as a "proposal of the Friends of the good officer," behind the back of the UN mediation. The FMLN quickly discovered that neither the United Nations nor the other Friends were aware of the initiative, and refused to sign. A chastised Venezuela returned to the fold of the Friends, which maintained their unity throughout the remaining negotiations.

Maintain a Flexible Approach

A mediator should take a strategic approach to engagement with Friends, recalling that the flexibility of the mechanism is one of its primary advantages. Groups of Friends have taken shape in multiple locations, maintained widely varying relations to the ongoing mediation, interacted with the mediator at different levels, and at times operated alongside other, larger groups in an attempt to counter some of the negative consequences of Friends' exclusivity.

Consider Multiple Locations

Multiple incarnations of a group of Friends are a reflection of the seriousness with which a process moves forward, with UN mediators, in particular, engaging regularly with counterparts in New York, in the field, and in the Friends' various capitals.

The primary locations of the Friends of El Salvador and Guatemala were New York and Mexico City; Friends in San Salvador and Guatemala City took shape as the negotiations in each process advanced. Groups were formed in Port-au-Prince and Tbilisi when peacekeeping operations were deployed to Haiti and Georgia, respectively.

In considering the benefits presented by different locations of a group of Friends, mediators should be aware that each location is likely to assume distinct characteristics. These include widely varying understandings of the conflict itself, as well as of the conflict parties, and differing capacities regarding national decision making and/or interaction with both conflict parties and other international partners.

Those Friends closest to the conflict itself enjoy advantages with regard to their knowledge of the immediate context within which the conflict takes place, as well as the likelihood of frequent interactions with state parties to a conflict and significant actors within civil society. However, they may have disadvantages, too. The primary identity of a Friend official is likely to be as bilateral ambassador accredited to a host government. A willingness to preserve this relationship may have implications for a Friend's ability to provide support to the peace process upon which the mediator is embarked. Moreover, such an ambassador may not have direct experience of other peace processes and thus be unprepared for the engagement that this may entail.

Friends at the capital level can contribute greater authority to a group's engagement in a peace process. They may be able either to make or to advocate for critical decisions regarding policy and the allotment of resources. They can also play a helpful role in educating the mediator regarding broader policy directions and discussions within the Friend state that might affect the mediator's efforts. Friend officials who are also representatives of a regional or multilateral organization will have a clear understanding of the broader international dynamics surrounding a conflict, and may be able to help the mediator ensure that these develop in support of the peace effort.

The Friends of the Secretary-General for Georgia developed groups with distinct identities in New York, Tbilisi, and Moscow, and also met at the capital level in Geneva. The different groups had different identities, with the Tbilisi group hindered by the simultaneous accreditation of its members to the Georgian government and that in Moscow impeded by the fact that busy ambassadors to Russia had many more pressing bilateral concerns than the Georgian-Abkhaz conflict. For these reasons, UN officials worked to ensure that some of the more difficult negotiations within the group took place in New York.

Encourage Coherence

In order to build and maintain a coordinated approach, a mediator needs to dedicate a considerable amount of time to briefing the various groupings of Friends. Although there may be occasions or subjects on which he or she wishes to engage a particular Friend in confidence, meeting the Friends as a group will save time, and contribute to the sense that they have embarked on a common venture. The timing of the briefings will be determined by the mediator. However, mediators have generally found it helpful to prioritize meetings both before and after new initiatives or rounds of negotiations with the conflict parties.

Mediators can encourage effective functioning of Friends in multiple locations by regularly interacting with the different individuals and groups concerned and encouraging them to report such encounters to one another. This can help build both expertise and coherence among the Friends.

During the Guatemala negations, the UN moderator Jean Arnault interacted frequently with the Friends in Mexico City, particularly before and after the many rounds of talks that were held there. These Friends reported back to their counterparts in New York and their capitals, facilitating Arnault's more infrequent engagement with these individuals, while also building a sense of commitment within each government.

Such networks can prove useful in a variety of ways. In the margins of talks, as well as in between them, Friends can reinforce the messages being delivered by the mediator within their own meetings with the parties. The mediator may find it useful to ask the Friends to issue public statements to support his or her efforts, welcoming an agreement reached or a step taken by the parties. At moments of particular tension or crisis—for example, in the final effort to reach an agreement or when conflict dynamics in the field suddenly escalate, requiring a new level of international attention—Friends can be mobilized in multiple locations.

During the crisis that developed in East Timor in the wake of the popular consultation held in August 1999, members of the core group in New York, at the capital level, and in Indonesia were in constant contact with one another. Existing channels of communication had created a degree of confidence among the core group members, and between their senior officials and Secretary-General Kofi Annan. These facilitated the role that Annan and the core group played in spearheading the international response, most notably through increasing pressure on President B. J. Habibie of Indonesia to accept the dispatch to East Timor of a multilateral force authorized by the UN Security Council.

Engage Different Levels

Under some circumstance, it may be possible and desirable to engage Friends at different levels in support of a peace process. Although a mediator's most frequent interlocutors will be ambassadors or special envoys of the Friend countries, on some occasions the mediator might consider enhancing the leverage of the Friends by reaching up to foreign ministers—or even a country's head of state. This might be accomplished by holding a ministerial meeting of the Friends in the margins of the UN General Assembly, or by encouraging discussion of the conflict on the sidelines of a presidential summit.

The heads of those states that made up the Friends of the Secretary-General for El Salvador were involved to an unusually high degree in the negotiations. During the first Ibero-American summit meeting, held in Guadalajara, Mexico, in mid-1991, the presidents of Colombia, Mexico, and Venezuela and the prime minister of Spain pressed Secretary-General Javier Pérez de Cuéllar to become more directly involved in the negotiations himself. This meeting both established the Friends as central actors in the process and consolidated the secretary-general's lead of the negotiating effort. From this point forward, the Friends—whose ambassadors Alvaro de Soto had until then preferred to meet with individually—began to meet with the United Nations as a group.

The extent to which engagement at this high level will be possible will vary greatly, depending on several factors, including the confidence in which the mediator is held by his or her own institution. The access to, and ear of, the UN secretary-general or relevant minister or head of state may prove helpful as a means both to galvanize Friends and, at critical moments, to impress the mediator's position upon the parties.

Consider Tiered Groups

Putting together groups of Friends can present difficult choices. A small mechanism can work with efficacy in close support of the mediator. But a larger and more inclusive—but necessarily unwieldy—group can confer greater legitimacy on the effort. Achieving a group whose membership adequately answers both demands—for efficacy and legitimacy—may be a challenge.

To meet this challenge, a mediator may wish to consider a tiered group, with a larger structure—which the Friends are likely to be members of as well—serving as a way to brief interested states on the progress of the peace process. Within a UN context, such groups serve a particularly useful purpose if the process in question is not yet on the agenda of a Security Council. Although discussion with a group of Friends is usually confidential, a larger group may provide a convenient venue in which the mediator can give a public, or semipublic, briefing on the progress of the political process, thus building support for the effort.

During the early months of 1999, UN officials working actively with the newly formed Core Group on East Timor encouraged the creation of a larger support group. This group met regularly, although less frequently than the core group. A flexible membership ensured access by all states interested in developments in East Timor and helped to prepare many of them to support the territory's transition to an independent state in the years that followed.

Work through Friends in Multilateral Institutions

The proliferation of groups of Friends and other mechanisms highlights the operational limits of multilateral structures—most prominently, the UN Security Council—charged with maintaining international peace and security. But it also reflects the structures' surprising resilience in a landscape of conflict resolution that has changed significantly since the end of the Cold War.

The workload of the Security Council is so heavy, and the membership—determined by the UN Charter more than sixty years ago—so obviously unrepresentative, that the creation of new groups brings welcome expertise and flexibility to its activities. In some cases, such groups assume a leading role in the council's decision making. In other cases, groups are kept at a greater distance from the workings of the council, while nevertheless providing a forum for engaging interested states from a conflict region and elsewhere.

A mediator working closely with a group of Friends should consider their potential for interaction with the UN Security Council, or a regional organization, to be a central element of their utility. But a mediator should also keep in mind that a strong group, dominated by permanent members of the council, can become a driving force within a political process. This can lead other members of the council to question whether it has usurped their authority or sidelined the mediator.

Over the years, elected members of the UN Security Council grumbled regularly about the tight control maintained by groups of Friends and contact groups over the council's decision-making process. The most frequent objects of criticism were the Friends of Georgia and Western Sahara and the Contact Group on the Balkans. In 2002, an ad hoc working group of the council on conflict prevention and resolution in Africa held several discussions on the establishment of groups of Friends and even arrived at a set of recommendations on their composition and attributions.[12] They were largely ignored.

Engage Friends on the UN Security Council

How a mediator engages Friends which are also members of the Security Council will depend on the extent to which they agree about the mediator's approach to the conflict. It will also reflect the positions assumed by other members of the Security Council.

In many peace processes, state actors that are parties to internal conflict—as well as other members of the Security Council concerned with broader questions of intervention or the precedent that might be set—resist the direct involvement of the Security Council before a peace operation is mandated. At times, Friends have played an active role in getting an issue on the agenda of the Security Council; at other times, they have resisted doing so.

After the military coup that ousted President Jean-Bertrand Aristide of Haiti in 1991, the four states (Canada, France, Venezuela, and the United States) that would become the Friends of the Secretary-General worked hard to bring the issue of Haiti to the UN Security Council and build support for a process of dialogue led by a UN special envoy. When this failed, successive Friends retained the leading role in driving Security Council action on Haiti.

By way of contrast, in 1994, during negotiations on Guatemala, the Friends overrode the recommendations from within the UN Secretariat for a

Security Council operation to monitor implementation of the peace agreement and instead insisted upon a mission mandated by the General Assembly. This was, at least in part, because the Latin American members of the Friends assumed that they would have a greater influence on developments in the latter forum.

A mediator should work closely with Friends to ensure that members of the council are informally briefed on the mediation's development. Friends may be well positioned to draft, or at least guide, statements by the council in support of the political and diplomatic efforts that are taking place outside it. In consultation with Friends, a mediator may also consider when a more formal briefing of the council as a whole would be appropriate, as well as how to engage the council itself directly. In addition to statements made, or measures (such as sanctions) threatened or imposed by the council, a visit by the council to the theater of conflict or crisis may prove helpful, both to inform the council members and as means of exerting leverage on the situation.

A visit by the Security Council to Dili in September 1999 allowed council members to see for themselves the devastation wrought upon the city during the postconsultation violence. In November 2004, during the final stages of the talks on Southern Sudan, the Security Council took the unusual step of holding a meeting in Nairobi. Speakers made strong calls to the conflict parties to reach a peace agreement by the end of the year. The meeting was addressed by both Ali Osman Taha, first vice president of the government of Sudan, and John Garang, leader of the SPLM/A, who reassured the members of the Security Council that the negotiations were nearing conclusion.

Once a peace operation has been mandated to oversee implementation of a peace agreement, the role of Friends within the Security Council will change. Although periodic reviews of progress on the ground and extensions of the peace operation's mandate assume a certain degree of predictability, the Friends will be well situated to provide the council with informed assessments of developments and advice at moments of crisis or reversal. They frequently will assume a privileged role within the drafting of the council's resolutions. Both mediators and those leading UN peace operations will therefore wish to prioritize ongoing consultation with the Friends.

Regional Organizations and Friends

Greater attention to conflict resolution within some regional organizations—most notably in Africa, but also in Europe and Latin America—has meant that these regions now frequently use groups of some kind. In Africa, these groups take myriad forms, with an increasing tendency to use international contact groups formally endorsed and/or led by the African Union as well as more flexible regional groupings (such as the regional facilitation on Burundi).

A critical aspect of these groups' utility is their ability to combine regional knowledge, legitimacy, and leverage with external resources and political influence. As such, they are important sounding boards for the various peacemakers involved, even as their size and the formality of their meetings, as well as the complex regional politics they reflect, can inhibit more flexible support. Although some of these groups have been extremely active (the International Contact Group on Guinea, formed in February 2009, met nine times in that year), many assume coordination and oversight functions rather than direct engagement with the political process.

By 2009, the International Contact Group on Somalia formed in 2006 had grown to thirty-one members and met regularly at the capital level; mediation and peacemaking remained the responsibility of the UN SRSG for Somalia, Ahmedou Ould Abdallah. Meanwhile, the International Contact Group on Madagascar provided support to a political effort led by the Southern African Development Cooperation (SADC)'s chief mediator, Joaquin Chissano, who headed a somewhat unwieldy Joint Mediation Team, consisting of the African Union, the International Organization of the Francophonie (OIF), SADC, and the United Nations.

In Latin America, groups of Friends of the Secretary-General of the Organization of American States have regularly been formed to facilitate diplomatic efforts to restore or further peace. In the early 2000s, a long-standing group of Friends of Haiti initially filled the vacuum when a UN peace operation was absent from the country. More recently, groups of Friends have been formed to address internal crises in Venezuela and Bolivia, and in mid-2009 a Dialogue Group was established to help address the crisis precipitated by the coup in Honduras.

For mediators, regional groups of Friends offer widely varying possibilities. Such groups have rarely enjoyed the close relationship to the mediation seen either in the UN context or in more informal settings. However, a mediator should seek to engage regional groups of Friends, when possible, to ensure legitimacy, resources, and support for his or her efforts.

STEP FIVE
Prepare for Implementation

In addition to the characteristics of the agreement reached between the conflict parties, success in laying the foundation for sustainable peace will depend on the interplay of three factors: the degree of hostilities between the warring factions, the extent of local capacities remaining after the war, and the amount of international assistance provided.[13] Influencing all three of these factors clearly lies beyond Friends or, indeed, any external actors. Yet the strategic coordination of international assistance to which the existence of a group of Friends seeks to contribute will be a critical component of the overall effort to reach and implement a peace agreement. Thus, preparing for implementation thus should be a central element of the mediator's engagement with a group of Friends, even though the mediator will recognize that the coordination required will necessarily involve a much wider range of actors than those which have been most closely involved in peacemaking.

The pressures of a peace negotiation in its final stages are extreme. A mediator will nevertheless need to remain forward looking in interactions with the conflict parties and external actors, and will need to be realistic in assessing the challenges ahead. Reaching a peace agreement is a considerable achievement. But in many respects, it is the beginning, not the end, of a long and difficult process. If the agreement provides for the establishment of a UN or other international security presence to assist in its implementation, all of the parties involved should have a clear sense of how to achieve the conditions that will eventually allow for its departure. In other words, the consolidation of national political institutions and processes.

Maximize Leverage in Advance of Reaching Agreement

The final stages of peace negotiations offer unprecedented opportunities for exerting leverage upon the conflict parties, which may be both consumed by the urgency of concluding an agreement and exhausted by the lengthy negotiation it has required. The influence of the mediator, both with the conflict parties and the various external actors involved, will be at its peak. The opportunity to put in place arrangements and resources for implementation should not be missed.

Involve Friends Directly in the Closing Stages

Friends can be involved directly in the closing stages of a mediation effort in a variety of ways. Their contacts with the conflict parties may intensify, as they seek advice and reassurance on the agreements they are preparing to sign. Friends can offer technical advice, but also the promise of sustained engagement and even specific guarantees of security.

During the final stages of the El Salvador negotiations, the security of FMLN commanders returning to the capital city of San Salvador was a critical issue. One element that helped overcome the FMLN's concern was the offer by the Friends that the five members of the organization's general command could each stay in the residence of a Friend ambassador for the first few weeks after their return.

Friends can be expected to make substantial contributions to the implementation effort. However, as the signing of a final agreement approaches, a mediator should be sensitive to the different interests and levels of commitment among the full panoply of external actors involved. The mediator will want to try to bind them as closely as possible to the agreement itself, and the priorities of the conflict parties that it represents. He or she will also want to ensure that the external actors' enthusiasm for and thus pressure upon the parties to reach agreement does not overtake the dynamics of the negotiations itself, leading to the signing of a flawed and unrealistic agreement. Such pressure can be difficult to resist, particularly in circumstances in which the external actors are also funding the negotiations.

External actors, including the United Kingdom and United States, involved in the final stages of the negotiations of the Darfur Peace Agreement

(DPA) in April and May 2006 imposed strict deadlines upon the African Union's mediation team and the various conflict parties. In retrospect, participants criticized this "deadline diplomacy" as being a factor that contributed to the flaws in the DPA, which was signed by only one of the Darfur armed movements and rapidly lost legitimacy.[14]

Mediators may find the closing stages of the talks complicated, as the parties to the conflict jockey for position in advance of the funding bonanza that is likely to follow the conclusion of the talks. Conflict parties will frequently perceive access to funding from the international community as part of their negotiating strategy, while potential donors may prioritize their own agendas.

In the closing stages of the Guatemala talks, the Friends agreed to host signing ceremonies for agreements on a definitive cease-fire in Oslo, on constitutional reform and the electoral regime in Stockholm, and on the reintegration of the URNG in Madrid, all in anticipation of the signing of the final peace agreement in Mexico City. The tour was designed to generate interest in Guatemala's needs as well as acknowledge the role of the Friends, but it did not prevent some Friends from prioritizing their own interests in implementation. Spain, for example, pursued a bilateral policy on public security that undermined the UN-led effort.

Mediators should encourage Friends and other external actors to impress upon the conflict parties the utility of establishing mechanisms to oversee implementation of the peace agreements reached. Ideally, these would involve both national and international actors and would meet regularly.

Seek Resource Commitments for Implementation

Implementation requires that extensive resources be applied simultaneously, and often over many years, to a dauntingly wide range of activities. In order to foster political stability, peace operations assume transitional security functions, which include guaranteeing cease-fires, demobilizing combatants, protecting civilians, and defusing tensions. They help implement the peace agreement or extend state authority through support to national political institutions and processes—or both. In recent years, they have also increasingly worked with others to establish the basis for secure development by supporting security sector reform and fostering rule of law institutions.[15]

These activities, which will be reinforced by early attention to economic, social, and institutional recovery, require ongoing mediation by the individual who heads the peace operation, but are also likely to extend beyond his or her mandate. They can be undertaken only through recourse to the widest range of instruments, agencies, and organizations at the disposal of the international community. A mediator may seek support from Friends in identifying needs and developing strategies to pursue them, and also in obtaining specific commitments to provide resources, which might include peacekeepers, technical expertise, and financial resources. But he or she will also need to work with a broad range of partners, including those in a position to mobilize resources, such as international financial institutions.

In numerous processes, the World Bank has assumed the lead in efforts to generate resources and coordinate donors for implementation. This may include convening Consultative Group meetings of multiple stakeholders, both before and after the peace agreement is signed. The World Bank, for example, convened thirteen donor coordination meetings on East Timor from September 1999 to April 2006 (after the independence of Timor Leste in 2002, these were called Timor Leste and Development Partner Meetings).

Adapt Structures and Strategy to New Circumstances

Usually, the role of the mediator culminates with the achievement of the peace agreement. The mediator may retain a role in oversight or follow-up of the implementation of the peace agreement, but the primary international responsibility for implementation will pass to others. When a peace operation is in place, its head may seek to work with existing structures—including a group of Friends—but he or she may also be presented with other implementation or monitoring groups created in the agreement, as well as a variety of donor mechanisms, both at the field level and capital based.

Work through Friends to Sustain Attention and Further Implementation

Despite these changed circumstances, sometimes a preexisting group of Friends—particularly if it has already been active at the level of local ambassadors—can prove to be an asset. A newly arrived SRSG or other official heading the peace operation should consider the utility of Friends as a source of expertise and a conduit to or vehicle of leverage on the government and other political forces.

In cases as varied as Cambodia, El Salvador, Haiti, and Mozambique, SRSGs have turned to Friends, or states configured as analogous core groups, in order to reinforce and multiply their own influence. In this way, they increase both their own impact and the international credibility of the United Nations' effort to sustain peace.

Exactly how Friends can help SRSGs and others will vary from case to case and according to the individual dispositions of the officials involved (some SRSGs work harder to cultivate Friends than others do). But Friends can fulfill a number of functions. These include exerting political influence on the parties to the conflict, sharing information regarding local developments and thinking in their capitals and in New York, acting as a sounding board for new ideas and initiatives, and helping to build and maintain consensus in the Security Council.

In Mozambique, the SRSG, Aldo Aiello, went so far as to share drafts of reports of the secretary-general to the Security Council with members of the Core Group in Maputo, many of which were also members of the Security Council. The practice assured smooth passage of the reports when they eventually arrived in New York, but would have been frowned upon by senior secretariat officials had they known about it.

In the context of efforts to improve the performance and transparency of UN peace operations, there has been increased discussion about the utility of headquarters-based groups of Friends as a way to foster greater involvement of troop-contributing countries.[16]

In 2000, years before troop contributors to MINUSTAH assumed prominent roles within the Friends of Haiti, a group called Friends of the UN Mission in Ethiopia and Eritrea (UNMEE) was formed on the initiative of the Netherlands. Making a return to peacekeeping for the first time since its traumatic experience in Srebrenica, the Netherlands was keen to ensure that troop contributors that did not sit on the UN Security Council remained involved in decision making that might affect their forces on the ground.

Seek Broad Coalitions for the Coordination of Assistance

Under some circumstances, governments may specifically reject the continuing existence of a group of Friends that was originally conceived as a way to facilitate communication between the mediation and conflict parties. Moreover, even without explicit rejection, as implementation advances, it is likely that the utility of a small and informal group of Friends, which worked closely with the mediator during the peacemaking phase, may be eclipsed by donor politics. An SRSG may therefore choose to prioritize bilateral contacts with representatives of key states alongside more infrequent meetings with broader coalitions for the coordination of assistance.

During implementation of the Guatemalan peace agreements, the Friends remained a useful mechanism for the coordination of UN engagement in New York, but quickly lost their influence within Guatemala. In time, the emergence of the Grupo de Dialogo (Dialogue Group), composed of the largest donors to the country, illustrated the stark fact that, as peacebuilding becomes the focus of the international effort, the leverage of international actors will be increasingly related to the power they wield as donors.

Once a settlement has been reached, the value of a mechanism to coordinate the key states involved is clearer than in the peacemaking stage—not least because the peace agreement provides, or should provide, a natural focus for their efforts. Indeed, studies of peace implementation have found that the use of a Friends group or other deliberate process to bring together key governments—generally inclusive of a greater number of states and organizations than the groups of Friends engaged in peacemaking—is a striking commonality among cases of successful implementation.[17]

Yet even in cases where such mechanisms are present, donor priorities and tensions between the political and economic demands made by the international community render such coordination notoriously difficult. Different strategies and mechanisms will need to be employed in different circumstances, with the broadest mechanisms of assistance coordination often meeting only outside the country in question. The SRSG or equivalent international actor should participate actively in the preparation of such meetings, even though they do not take place under his or her authority.

Closer in function to ongoing processes of mediation are the variety of groups established to channel the efforts of external actors toward implementation in the field. These mechanisms are not usually created as donor coordination mechanisms. But neither are they equivalent to the peacemaking groups of Friends. They are larger and more formally constituted, with their composition and functions often provided for in the peace agreement itself.

In the DRC, where peacemaking had been hindered by the active participation in the conflict by states of the region as well as competing allegiances in the Security Council, a group such as CIAT had its own logic and purpose. The limitations of this group—also evident in the core group created for Haiti in 2004—included those natural to its size, as well as government sensitivity regarding the intervention it represented as the process advanced beyond the point where it could willingly accept international tutelage.

Groups of more than a dozen members represent forums ill suited to address the substantive differences held by their members on the complex process in which they are engaged. But peacemakers and implementers may still wish to consider their potential to build consensus among the key members of the international community and, on the basis of that consensus, encourage forward momentum in the complex transitions under way. The existence of such mechanisms will obviously not prevent the development of alternative, more informal, channels for consultation with key partners.

Conclusion

This handbook has presented groups of Friends as a mechanism of potential utility to peacemakers as they consider the very considerable challenge presented by the effective engagement of external actors. The handbook has not, however, presented groups of Friends as a panacea. Instead, it has suggested that the formation of a group of Friends is worthy of careful consideration but has also cautioned that a group will require care and attention before its establishment, as well as in its maintenance.

Experience reveals that there will be many circumstances in which, after such consideration, a peacemaker will choose against the formation of a defined group of Friends. This handbook seeks to encourage and facilitate the rigorous analysis of the potential—and risks—presented to a mediation by the various external actors in the region of the conflict and in the wider international community. Some of their intentions with regard to the peace effort may, as we have seen, be friendly, while others may be anything but.

The extent to which a peacemaker may be empowered to orchestrate such actors will vary greatly but is never likely to be as much as he or she might wish. In addition, the situation is likely to be a good deal more complex and murkier than can be presented in a book. This handbook has nevertheless suggested some core elements that should be maintained as a mediator considers whether and how to work with a group of Friends.

Four elements in particular stand out. The first is that external actors cannot be ignored. A strategy for their engagement may or may not involve a group of Friends, but the process of the development of such a strategy will be useful to a mediator whether or not a group structure is deemed appropriate, both as a means of making use of external partners' leverage and resources, and as a means of countering unhelpful external involvement. Second, such a strategy should prioritize a careful analysis of potential Friends' knowledge, relationships, and influence, as well as their readiness to support a mediation led by another. Third, strategic coordination does not come easily. The development and maintenance of relationships with external actors, whether convened as Friends or not, requires time, patience, and flexibility, in accordance with the gradual evolution of the peace process. Finally, mediators should recall that peacemaking is a long-term activity, in which sustained investment in individual partners or groups of Friends may bring with it many, and in some cases unsuspected, benefits.

Notes

1. This handbook draws on research previously conducted by the author and published in Teresa Whitfield, *Friends Indeed? The United Nations, Groups of Friends and the Resolution of Conflict* (Washington, D.C.: United States Institute of Peace Press, 2007). Additional research was conducted in parallel to that conducted for Teresa Whitfield, *External actors in mediation: Dilemmas and options for mediators,* Mediation Practice Series I, (Geneva: Centre for Humanitarian Dialogue, February 2010)

2. See, for example, George Downs and Stephen John Stedman, "Evaluation Issues in Peace Implementation," in *Ending Civil Wars: The Implementation of Peace Agreements,* ed. Stephen John Stedman, Donald Rothchild, and Elizabeth M. Cousens, 43–69 (Boulder, CO: Lynne Rienner, 2002).

3. See Robert Ricgliano, ed., *Choosing to Engage: Armed Groups and Peace Processes,* Accord Issue 16 (London: Conciliation Resources, 2005).

4. UN press briefing by special envoy to Afghanistan, October 20, 1999.

5. See Chester A. Crocker, "Peacemaking and Mediation: Dynamics of a Changing Field," *Coping with Crisis,* Working Paper Series (New York: International Peace Academy, 2007) for a succinct discussion of this subject.

6. The group was established in 1993 as the Friends of Georgia and became the Friends of the UN Secretary-General for Georgia in 1997. Although its core membership remained France, Germany, Russia, the United Kingdom, and the United States, it was joined in New York only by Ukraine, Bulgaria, and Slovakia during their respective terms as elected members of the Security Council in 2000–01, 2002–03, and 2006–07.

7. Alvaro de Soto, interviewed by Jean Krasno, April 9, 1996, Yale/UN Oral History Project.

8. In 2008 and 2009, the Norwegian Refugee Council provided the United Nations' Mediation Support Unit with a standby team of mediation experts to supplement its own in-house capacity.

9. Jean Arnault, interview conducted by Connie Peck as part of the United Nations Institute for Training and Research Programme for Briefing and Debriefing Special and Personal Representatives and Envoys of the UN Secretary-General. Consulted with the permission of Jean Arnault.

10. The nongovernmental organization Independent Diplomat offers diplomatic advice to marginalized and disadvantaged governments and political groups who have difficulty articulating their interests and gaining access to diplomatic forums and international negotiations. Its clients include the Kosovar Albanians, the Polisario Front, Somaliland, and Turkish Cyprus.

11. David Hannay, *Cyprus: The Search for a Solution* (London: I. B. Taurus, 2005), 119.

12. Annex to the letter dated August 29, 2002, from the permanent representative of Mauritius to the president of the Security Council, S/2002/979, of August 30, 2002.
13. Michael W. Doyle and Nicholas Sambanis, *Making War and Building Peace: United Nations Peace Operations* (Princeton, NJ, and Oxford: Oxford University Press, 2006).
14. Laurie Nathan, "The Making and Unmaking of the Darfur Peace Agreement," and Alex de Waal, "Darfur's Deadline: The Final Days of the Abuja Peace Process," in Alex de Waal, ed., *War in Darfur and the Search for Peace,* 245–66 and 267–83 (Harvard, MA: Global Equity Initiative, Harvard University, 2007).
15. On the multiple challenges facing UN peace operations, see Bruce Jones, Richard Gowan, and Jake Sherman, "Building on Brahimi: Peacekeeping in an Age of Strategic Uncertainty," NYU Center on International Cooperation, April 2009, www.peacekeepingbestpractices.unlb.org/pbps/Library/CIC%20New%20Horizon%20Think%20Piece.pdf.
16. Ibid.
17. Bruce D. Jones, "The Challenges of Strategic Coordination," in *Ending Civil Wars,* ed. Stedman et al., 99.

Acknowledgments

The author would like to thank Marie Pace, formerly of the United States Institute of Peace, and A. Heather Coyne and Nigel Quinney, the editors of *The Peacemaker's Toolkit* series, for their assistance and guidance in seeing this publication to completion. She would also like to express her gratitude to the anonymous reviewers, whose perceptive observations greatly improved its clarity, and to the mediators, diplomats, and representatives of conflict parties who have over the years shared their experiences of groups of Friends with her.

About the Author

Teresa Whitfield is a senior fellow and adviser on UN strategy at New York University's Center on International Cooperation and a senior adviser to the Centre for Humanitarian Dialogue in Geneva, with responsibility for liaison with the United Nations. From 2005 to 2008, she was director of the Conflict Prevention and Peace Forum, a program of the Social Science Research Council that facilitates access by UN officials to outside sources of expertise on countries in conflict or crisis. In 1995–2000 she worked as an official within the United Nations' Department of Political Affairs. She is a member of the board of trustees of Conciliation Resources and of the advisory board of the Conflict Prevention and Peace Forum. Her publications include *Friends Indeed? The United Nations, Groups of Friends, and the Resolution of Conflict* (Washington, D.C.: United States Institute of Peace Press, 2007).

About the United States Institute of Peace

The United States Institute of Peace is an independent, nonpartisan institution established and funded by Congress. The Institute provides analysis, training, and tools to help prevent, manage, and end violent international conflicts, promote stability, and professionalize the field of peacebuilding.

Chairman of the Board: J. Robinson West

Vice Chairman: George E. Moose

President: Richard H. Solomon

Executive Vice President: Tara Sonenshine

Chief Financial Officer: Michael Graham

Board of Directors

J. Robinson West (Chair), Chairman, PFC Energy, Washington, D.C.

George E. Moose (Vice Chairman), Adjunct Professor of Practice, The George Washington University

Anne H. Cahn, Former Scholar in Residence, American University

Chester A. Crocker, James R. Schlesinger Professor of Strategic Studies, School of Foreign Service, Georgetown University

Ikram U. Khan, President, Quality Care Consultants, LLC

Kerry Kennedy, Human Rights Activist

Stephen D. Krasner, Graham H. Stuart Professor of International Relations, Stanford University

Jeremy A. Rabkin, Professor, George Mason School of Law

Judy Van Rest, Executive Vice President, International Republican Institute

Nancy Zirkin, Executive Vice President, Leadership Conference on Civil Rights

Members Ex Officio

Michael H. Posner, Assistant Secretary of State for Democracy, Human Rights, and Labor

James N. Miller, Principal Deputy Under Secretary of Defense for Policy

Ann E. Rondeau, Vice Admiral, U.S. Navy; President, National Defense University

Richard H. Solomon, President, United States Institute of Peace (nonvoting)